YOUR MEDIEVAL

Homework Helper

by Susie Hodge
Consultants: Richard Tames and Dr. Andrew Reynolds

ticktock MEDIA

How to use this book

Each topic in this book is clearly labelled and contains all these components:

Topic heading

Power

Words to use in your project
barons (po
governmen
managing a

Introduction to the topic

'Medieval' is the name given to the period of European history that lasted from about 1000–1500. The medieval period is also called the Middle Ages. In medieval times, KINGS ruled most of the larger states of Europe. Most kings and queens still had to defend themselves against rebellions as not everyone agreed that they should be in control of the people. Not all of the medieval kings were good leaders. Some were lazy and weak while others were harsh and cruel.

Sub-topic 1 offers complete information about one aspect of the topic

BARONS

Next in rank to the king or queen were the **BARONS**. These wealthy men controlled large armies of knights to help the king fight his enemies. Sometimes the barons rebelled and overthrew their king. In 1215, the barons made King John add his seal to an agreement that they had written, called the 'Great Charter' (or 'Magna Carta'), to stop him being so

Source – Magna Carta, England, 1215

A ROYAL LINE

After William of Normandy defeated Harold at the Battle of Hastings in 1066, he became king of England. When he died, his sons carried on his ROYAL LINE.

The only medieval queen of England was William's granddaughter Matilda, although she was never officially crowned. Stephen, her cousin, became king instead. Many did not believe he had the right to the throne while others did not want a **WOMAN RULER**. This division caused a civil war. A source from the period describes life at the time:

'... some of the people disgustingly devoured the flesh of dogs and horses; others appeased their insatiable hunger with the garbage of

uncooked herbs and roots; many, in all parts, sunk under the severity of the famine and died in heaps ... Thus the whole aspect of England presented a scene of calamity and sorrow, misery and oppression.'

Stephen died in 1154 and Matilda's son ruled next. He was Henry II, the first of a long line of Anglo-French or 'Plantagenet' kings.

This scene from the Bayeux Tapestry shows the death of Harold at the battle of Hastings in 1066.

Source – Chronicle of Henry, Archdeacon of Huntingdon, England, c. 1080–1160

POWER GLOSSARY

calamity	Terrible situation
civil war	A war fought between rivals in the same country
famine	Servere shortage of food
feudal system	When land is held by people in return for their hard work and loyalty
fedility	Loyalty
insatiable	Never satisfied
Knight	A high-ranking soldier

See also: Country Life 10–11; Crime and Punishment 20–2

Choose a word from the Keyword Contents on page 3. Then, turn to the correct page and look for your word in BOLD CAPITALS. This will take you straight to the information you need

4

The Glossary explains the meaning of any unusual or difficult words appearing on these two pages

Copyright © *ticktock* Entertainment Ltd 2004

First published in Great Britain in 2004 by *ticktock* Media Ltd.,

Unit 2, Orchard Business Centre, North Farm Road, Tunbridge Wells, Kent, TN2 3XF

We would like to thank: Meme Ltd and Egan-Reid Ltd for their help with this book.

ISBN 1 86007 542 8 HB

ISBN 1 86007 536 3 PB

Printed in China

A CIP catalogue record for this book is available from the British Library.

Keyword Contents

Sub-topic 2 offers complete information about one aspect of the topic

Some suggested words to use in your project

The Case Study is a closer look at a famous person, artefact or building that relates to the topic

monarchs (kings and queens)
nobility (rich and powerful people)

overthrow (remove from power)
peasants (poor farmers)

Each photo or illustration is described and discussed in its accompanying text

CASE STUDY

The Feudal System

The barons made King John seal the Great Charter in 1215 as a promise to be just to his people.

. This was the o set out the REEDOMS of One of the rights harter stated: m we have sessed of lands, r rights, without ent of his equals, store these.'

William I introduced the 'FEUDAL SYSTEM' to England. It was a system where everyone knew their place in society. It worked like this: the king, who originally owned all the land, gave some of it to the church and the barons. In return for large blocks of land, the barons promised to fight for the king. The barons then lent some of their land to the knights if they too promised to fight for the king. The knights then lent some of their land to the common people, promising to look after them if they looked after the land. People had to take 'oaths of fidelity' where they promised to abide by the rules of the feudal system. Here is an extract from one:

'I promise on my faith that I will in future be faithful to count William, and will observe my homage to him completely against all persons in good faith and without deceit.'

This illumination from 1469 shows Jean de Sainte-Maure making the oath of fidelity to become a baron.

Captions clearly explain what is in the picture

Source – 'Homage and Fealty to the Count of Flanders' from Galbert de Bruges, Chronicle of the Death of Charles the Good, Belgium, 1127

harter) document people's rights of ruling en to the Anglo- of kings and ing the Middle Ages nting against mbol stamped into ers or documents

26–27

Other pages in the book that relate to what you have read here are listed in this bar

At the bottom of each section, a reference bar tells you where the quote has come from

Power

'Medieval' is the name given to the period of European history that lasted from about 1000–1500. The medieval period is also called the Middle Ages. In medieval times, KINGS ruled most of the larger states of Europe. Most kings and queens still had to defend themselves against rebellions as not everyone agreed that they should be in control of the people. Not all of the medieval kings were good leaders. Some were lazy and weak while others were harsh and cruel.

A ROYAL LINE

After William of Normandy defeated Harold at the Battle of Hastings in 1066, he became king of England. When he died, his sons carried on his ROYAL LINE.

The only medieval queen of England was William's granddaughter Matilda, although she was never officially crowned. Stephen, her cousin, became king instead. Many did not believe he had the right to the throne while others did not want a **WOMAN RULER.** This division caused a civil war. A source from the period describes life at the time:

'... some of the people disgustingly devoured the flesh of dogs and horses; others appeased their insatiable hunger with the garbage of uncooked herbs and roots; many, in all parts, sunk under the severity of the famine and died in heaps ... Thus the whole aspect of England presented a scene of calamity and sorrow, misery and oppression.'

Stephen died in 1154 and Matilda's son ruled next. He was Henry II, the first of a long line of Anglo-French or 'Plantagenet' kings.

This scene from the Bayeux Tapestry shows the death of Harold at the battle of Hastings in 1066.

Source – Chronicle of Henry, Archdeacon of Huntingdon, England, c. 1080–1160

Words to use in your project

barons *(powerful lords)*
government *(group of people managing a country)*
monarchs *(kings and queens)*
nobility *(rich and powerful people)*
overthrow *(remove from power)*
peasants *(poor farmers)*

BARONS

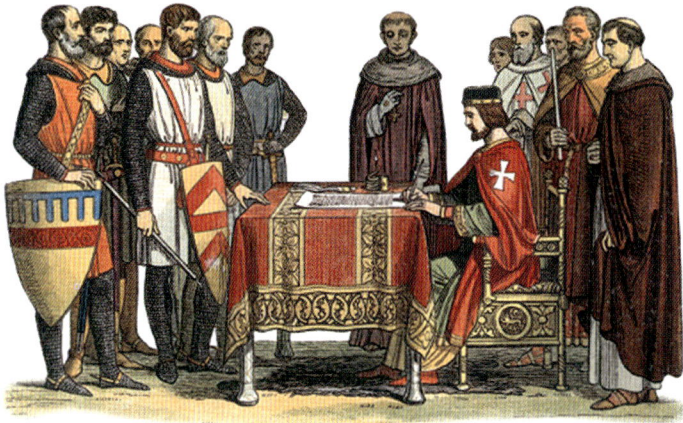

The barons made King John seal the Great Charter in 1215 as a promise to be fair to his people.

Next in rank to the king or queen were the **BARONS**. These wealthy men controlled large armies of knights to help the king fight his enemies. Sometimes the barons rebelled and overthrew their king. In 1215, the barons made King John add his seal to an agreement that they had written, called the 'Great Charter' (or 'Magna Carta'), to stop him being so harsh and greedy. This was the first document to set out the **RIGHTS AND FREEDOMS** of English people. One of the rights included in the charter stated:

'To any man whom we have deprived or dispossessed of lands, castles, liberties, or rights, without the lawful judgement of his equals, we will at once restore these.'

Source – Magna Carta, England, 1215

Power Glossary

calamity	Terrible situation	**Magna Carta**	(or Great Charter) Document that set out people's rights
civil war	A war fought between rivals in the same country	**oppression**	Harsh way of ruling
famine	Severe shortage of food	**Plantagenet**	Name given to the Anglo-French line of kings and queens during the Middle Ages
feudal system	When land is held by people in return for their hard work and loyalty		
fidelity	Loyalty	**rebellion**	People fighting against their rulers
insatiable	Never satisfied	**seal**	Person's symbol stamped into wax on letters or documents
knight	A high-ranking soldier		

See also: Country Life 10–11; Crime and Punishment 20–21; The Crusades 22–23; Buildings 26–27

CASE STUDY

The Feudal System

William I introduced the **'FEUDAL SYSTEM'** to England. It was a system where everyone knew their place in society. It worked like this: the king, who originally owned all the land, gave some of it to the church and the barons. In return for large blocks of land, the barons promised to fight for the king. The barons then lent some of their land to the knights if they too promised to fight for the king. The knights then lent some of their land to the common people, promising to look after them if they looked after the land. People had to take 'oaths of fidelity' where they promised to abide by the rules of the feudal system. Here is an extract from one:

'I promise on my faith that I will in future be faithful to count William, and will observe my homage to him completely against all persons in good faith and without deceit.'

This illumination from 1469 shows Jean de Sainte-Maure making the oath of fidelity to become a baron.

Source – 'Homage and Fealty to the Count of Flanders' from Galbert de Bruges, Chronicle of the Death of Charles the Good, Belgium, 1127

Religion

People believed that GOD controlled everything. The dominant religion in much of Europe was CHRISTIANITY, which was split into Orthodox Christianity in Eastern Europe and Catholicism in Western Europe. Church leaders such as bishops and archbishops played leading roles in the government. The archbishop was the chief bishop who ruled over the bishops in a wide area. Bishops, who were often wealthy and came from noble families, ruled over groups of parishes called 'dioceses'.

PEOPLE IN THE CHURCH

PRIESTS led the church service, called the 'Mass', in towns and villages throughout the land. People went to priests to confess their sins and the priest could forgive them on behalf of God.

Like priests, **MONKS** and **NUNS** also chose to devote their lives to God – living in religious communities called monasteries and convents. Like priests, neither monks nor nuns were allowed to marry. They also took vows to own nothing and to do whatever the abbot or abbess told them. Sundays were spent praying and all other days were divided into prayer, study and work. Work could be copying manuscripts and decorating them with illuminated letters, cooking, cleaning or working in the fields. Some ran schools or cared for the sick and others simply spent their lives praying. St Francis founded an order of **FRIARS** called the Franciscans. Unlike many other religious orders, the Franciscans did not

Many people at the time could not read or write, but most religious figures could, as represented by St Peter in this 13th century Italian painting.

have to live confined to monestaries. St Francis wrote this advice to fellow friars:

'I worked with my hands, and want to do so still. And I definitely want all the other brothers to work at some honest job. Those who don't know how should learn, not because they want to receive wages but as an example and to avoid idleness.'

Source – The Testament of St Francis, Italy, 1226

HEAVEN AND HELL

People believed that when a person died, they went to 'purgatory' where God decided whether they should be sent to **HEAVEN** or **HELL.** To move from purgatory to heaven, the person had to have lived an honest life. Medieval visions of hell were painted on church walls to remind people to be good. The Italian writer Dante Alighieri wrote an epic poem called *The Divine Comedy* which gave very vivid descriptions of hell, like this one:

'*These wretches, who ne'er lived, Went on in nakedness, and sorely stung; By wasps and hornets, which bedew'd their cheeks; With blood, that, mix'd with tears, dropp'd to their feet, And by disgustful worms was gather'd there.*'

Images of hell like the one in this 15th century French painting appeared on the walls of churches to warn people about hell.

Source – Dante Alighieri, The Divine Comedy, Italy, 1313

Religion Glossary

abbot (or abbess)	Head of a monastery (or convent)	**Orthodox**	Traditional form of Christianity in Eastern Europe
diocese	Group of parishes that a bishop is in charge of	**purgatory**	Waiting and suffering before a person entered heaven
epic	Long poem	**wattle & daub**	Twigs woven together and coated with a mixture of mud or clay, horsehair and straw
illuminated manuscript	Decorated book		
Mass	Catholic church service		

CASE STUDY

Churches

The **CHURCH** was always situated right in the middle of the town or village as it was the most important part of medieval life. Every day, people could hear the church bells ringing on every hour – from wherever they were. This was supposed to remind people of their duty to God. When a person was born they would be baptised in the church, then they would worship at Mass throughout their lives. They would get married in the church and then, at the end of their lives, they would be buried in the churchyard. Rich people might be buried under finely carved stone monuments, while the poor were buried in unmarked graves. The church was usually built from stone when most other buildings were made of wood or wattle and daub.

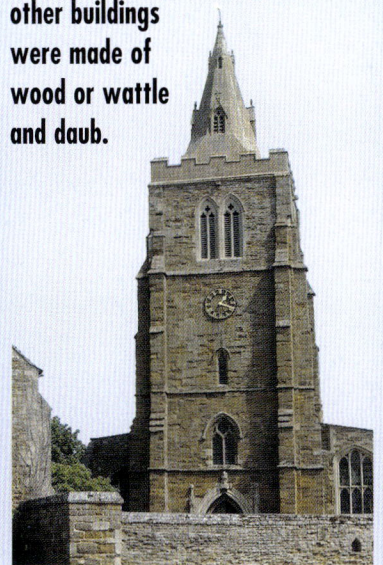

The church was the biggest building in the medieval town. This one is in the English town of Lyddington.

See also: Health and Medicine 16–17; Art 24–25; Buildings 26–27; Penance and Pilgrimages 30–31

Town Life

In medieval times, there were far fewer towns than there are today and not many big cities. Some medieval cities had proper drainage systems, although in most towns water had to be carried to each house from wells. The towns were busy places. Farmers herded livestock or drove carts through the streets. People went to towns to buy and sell goods at the MARKETS, and then gradually more people moved to the towns – often to learn the CRAFTS or trades that were becoming popular.

MARKETS

Everything – from shoes to furniture – was made by hand. The TRADESPEOPLE who made these included weavers, dyers, candlemakers, carpenters, blacksmiths, tailors and goldsmiths.

Boys and girls began learning these skills from a young age and were known as 'apprentices'. Most peasants went to market every week in their nearest town. They sold home-produced food, such as vegetables or eggs. Some set up takeaway food stalls and others sold goods bought from craftspeople or merchants. Markets had a reputation for being unholy places, as described in this account:

'They are held on feast days, and men miss thereby the divine office and the sermon and even disobey the precept of hearing Mass, and attend these meetings against the Church's commands.

Sometimes, too, they are held in graveyards and other holy places. Frequently you will hear men swearing there: "By God I will not give you so much for it," or "By God I will not take a smaller price," or "By God it is not worth so much as that" ... sometimes, too, quarrels happen and violent disputes ...'.

Craftspeople and traders sold all sorts of things at the market, such as: food, pots, shoes and hats.

Source – Humbert de Romans, On Markets & Fairs, France, c. 1270

DAILY LIFE

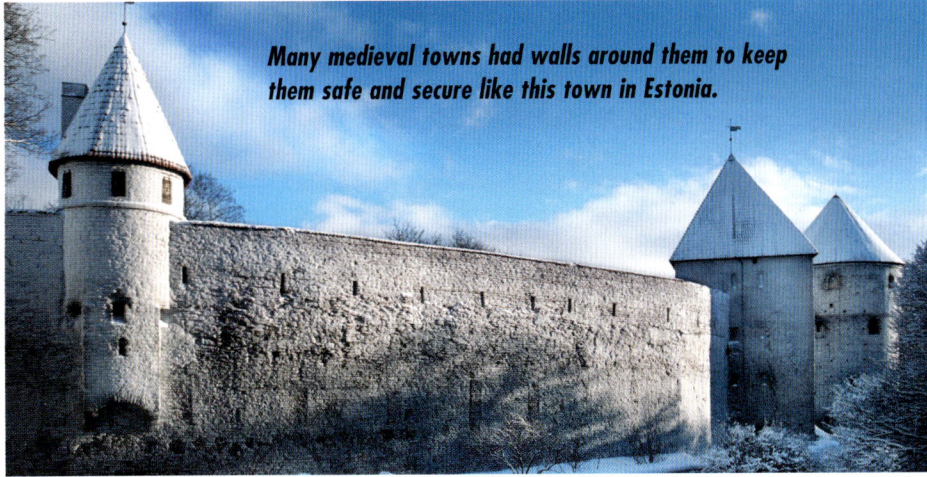

Many medieval towns had walls around them to keep them safe and secure like this town in Estonia.

Many medieval towns were surrounded by stone **WALLS. STREETS** were usually narrow, cramped and dirty, especially on market days when traders, shoppers, beggars, thieves, farmers and animals all passed by. We can learn about the layout of medieval markets by looking at street names that still exist, such as: Baker Street, Tanner Street, Pudding Lane and Fish Row.

For example, in Oxford, Beef Lane is beside the southern gate of the town, so historians believe that this was where live cattle were brought to town and slaughtered. Many streets had shops along the sides that opened at the front to sell goods directly to customers. As most people couldn't read, shop signs had to have pictures in them. For example, a boot would hang above a cobbler's shop.

Town Life Glossary

apprentices	Children who learn craft skills in the home of a master-craftsman
divine	To do with God or religion
fortress	A strong structure that is secure against attack
livestock	Farm animals
merchants	People who buy or sell goods, often from foreign countries
sermon	Talk on a religious subject
tradespeople	People who traded with others, e.g. shopkeepers
traitors	People who carry out crimes against the monarch or country

CASE STUDY

London

The city of London grew up on the banks of the River Thames. Like other towns, a high stone wall surrounded it. Yet despite being the largest city in medieval England, you could walk from one side of the city to the other in 20 minutes. The **TOWER OF LONDON** was built in the 1070s as a fortress, palace and **PRISON**. Between 1176 and 1209, a 19-arch stone bridge was built across the Thames. It was named London Bridge. It had houses, shops and a chapel on it and it held fairs and markets where traitors' heads were displayed after they had been chopped off.

The Tower of London was built in the 1070s as a fortress, palace and prison.

See also: Death 12–13; Crime and Punishment 20–21; Buildings 26–27; Trade and Craft 28–29

Country Life

Nine out of ten people in medieval England were PEASANTS who lived in the countryside. Most worked on the land as part of the feudal system and paid the church a tax called a 'tithe'. Peasants usually worked extremely hard. There were many jobs to do all year round on the medieval farm, such as looking after animals, ploughing and harvesting.

FARMING

Fields around medieval villages did not look like most fields today because FARMING was done in a different way.

This painting from the Italian school in the 14th century shows a peasant woman feeding grain to roosters.

Most fields were 'open' – without hedges or fences. Peasants grew **CROPS** such as wheat, oats, peas, beans and barley. **ANIMALS** were kept on the manor and looked after by the villagers. These included oxen, cows, sheep, goats, pigs, geese and hens. Sheep were kept for their wool and most peasants sheared them in the summer months. Other animals were kept for meat, milk and eggs as well as their skins, which were tanned and made into clothing and other goods. We know much about medieval farming from surviving texts like this one offering advice to farmers:

'When your lambs are yeaned let the shepherd take away the wool about the teats, for often it happens that the wool adheres to the mouths of the lambs from the teats, and they swallow it, and it remains in their stomachs, and thereby many have died.'

Source – Walter of Henley, Treatise on Husbandry, England, c. 1270

Words to use in your project

agriculture (farming)
boundaries (limits of an area)
harvesting (gathering crops)

labour (work)
peasant (poor farmer or farm labourer)

ploughing (turning over the land for farming)
rustic (life in the country)

HARD WORK

Peasants worked hard on the land and there was work to do nearly every day of the year.

All farm work was done by hand using simple **TOOLS**. Most jobs involved very hard work like hoeing crops, shearing sheep, carrying manure, ploughing and harvesting. Peasants worked hard every day except Sundays and holy days, whatever the weather. Most villages had a blacksmith, a carpenter and others with special jobs. Most country folk, however, were terribly **POOR** and hungry. Many caught wild animals from the lord's estate but if they were caught, they would be severely punished. An anonymous document from the period describes how much a farm labourer should be paid:

'You can well have three acres weeded for a penny, and an acre of meadow mown for fourpence, and an acre of waste meadow for threepence-halfpenny, and an acre of meadow turned and raised for a penny-halfpenny, and an acre of waste for a penny-farthing.'

Source – Walter of Henley, Treatise on Husbandry, England, c. 1270

Country Life Glossary

adheres	Sticks to	**sustenance**	Well-being
farthing	Coin worth quarter of a penny	**tithe**	Tax which medieval people had to pay the village priest: one tenth of their farm produce
halfpenny	Coin with half a penny		
manor	Block of land under the control of one lord	**yeaned**	Probably an old-fashioned word for 'weaned'
shearing	Cutting the wool off sheep		

See also: Power 4–5; Death 12–13; Buildings 26–27; Trade and Craft 28–29

CASE STUDY

This is a 12th–13th century manor house in Shropshire, England where the lord and lady would have lived.

The Manor House

The **MANOR HOUSE** was a large house with land where the lord and lady of the manor lived. In return for the right to live in the manor house, the lord would have been loyal to an even greater landowner – the baron. The baron would sometimes send someone to watch over the running of the manor. Here are some of one baron's expectations:

'... if there be any cheating in the sowing, or plowing, or reaping, he shall easily see it. And he must cause all the meadows and several pastures to be measured by acres, and thereby can one know the cost, and how much hay is necessary every year for the sustenance of the manor.'

The lord expected the villagers to work on his land in return for a house and land of their own.

Source – The Seneschaucy, England, c. 1270

Death

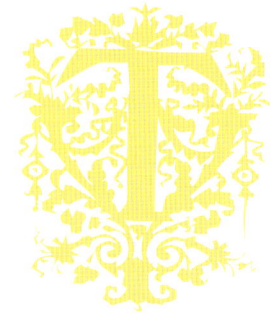

The average LIFE EXPECTANCY for people in the Middle Ages was between 30 and 35 years old. War, famine and diseases claimed thousands of lives. Widespread POVERTY meant that many houses were overcrowded and that people were living on the streets. All these things contributed to disease and early death. From studying their skeletons, archaeologists have learnt that many medieval peasants had worn out joints and deformities caused by many years of hard work. The bones also show us how people died, often from infectious diseases like the plague.

SHORT LIVES

The most common causes of death were dirty water and bad hygiene – especially in the crowded, dirty towns. Poor diet was another big reason.

A low intake of dairy products meant that immunity was low. It was also quite common for a newborn baby and/or its mother to die during **CHILDBIRTH** because of bad hygiene. Very few things – people's bodies, the streets, houses – were clean, and certainly not by today's standards. Other common diseases included tuberculosis, dysentery and smallpox. There was no proper system for getting rid of sewage like we have today. Filth flowed in the ditches along the roads, and people sometimes went to the toilet out of their windows if they couldn't be bothered going to the privy! In 1349, Edward III made a complaint to the Mayor of London about the dirty streets of London being directly related to the spread of disease:

A common 14th century scene: a doctor and priest read a dying man his last rites.

'Cause the human faeces and other filth lying in the streets and lanes in the city to be removed with all speed to places far distant, so that no greater cause of mortality may arise from such smells.'

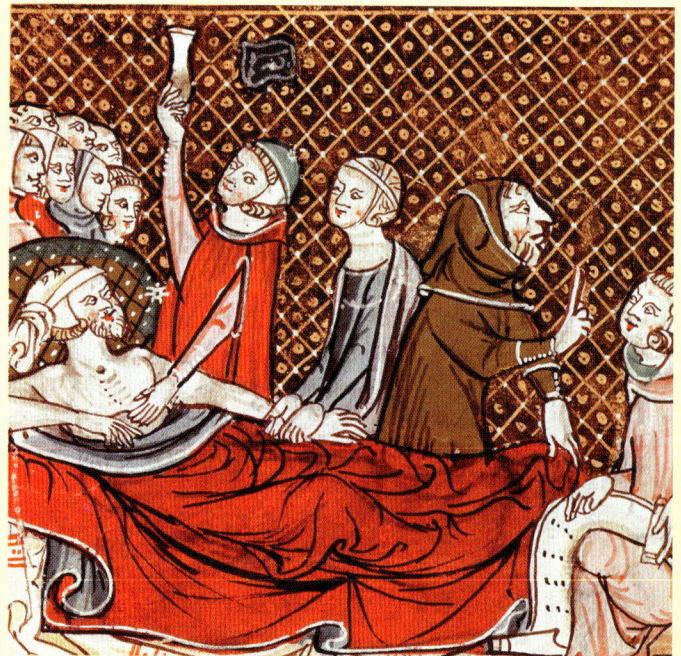

Source – Edward III, Letter to Mayor of London, England, 1349

Words to use in your project

contagious (disease that people pass to others)
epidemic (widespread disease)
execution (carrying out a sentence of death)
flouted (rejected)
hygiene (cleanliness)
poverty (being poor)
treachery (betrayal)

THE PLAGUE

Between 1347 and 1349, the 'bubonic **PLAGUE**' or 'Black Death' killed about one in three people across Europe. It spread quickly and no one knew how to **CURE** it. Few people who caught it survived for more than about three days. Many people believed that the Black Death was a punishment from God. A source from the period describes what happened when a person caught the disease:

This French painting from 1499 shows St. Sebastian appearing to victims of the plague.

'Many would meet their end in the public streets both day and night, and many others, who met their ends in their own houses, would first come to the attention of their neighbors because of the stench of their rotting corpses more than anything else; and with these and others all dying, there were corpses everywhere.'

Source – Boccaccio, The Decameron, Italy, 1348

Death Glossary

bubonic plague Disease affecting huge numbers of people (also called the 'Black Death')

chrism Type of holy oil dabbed on foreheads of religious figures

consecrated Something made sacred

famine People suffering from barely any food

immunity Body's natural defense against disease and illness

impious Naughty or disrespectful

life expectancy The normal length of time a person will live

privy An outdoor room where people went to the toilet

CASE STUDY

Murder!

In 1162, Henry II chose his close friend, Thomas Becket to become the Archbishop of Canterbury. Becket believed this meant that his duty to the Church must now come before his duty to the king. This made the king angry causing some of the his knights to go to Canterbury, where they **MURDERED** Becket on the steps of the altar in the Cathedral. An eyewitness account reported Becket's death:

'... the impious knight, fearing that [Thomas] would be saved by the people and escape alive, suddenly set upon him and, shaving off the summit of his crown which the sacred chrism consecrated to God, he wounded the sacrificial lamb of God in the head ...'.

This picture from a medieval manuscript shows Thomas Becket turning his back on royal power.

Source – Edward Grim, The Murder of Thomas Becket, England, 1170

See also: Religion 6–7; Town Life 8–9; Country Life 10–11; Health and Medicine 16–17

Eating and Drinking

Medieval people had quite an UNHEALTHY diet. For instance, they believed that fresh fruit was harmful. Rich people could afford a wide range of food, such as dried fruit, meats, sauces, puddings, nuts and cream. Peasants ate the food that they grew. We know what people ate from the remains of their meals found on archaeological sites as, to get rid of their rubbish, people would throw it into pits behind their houses.

WHAT THEY ATE

The rich ate fresh MEAT, such as venison, chicken and goose. Salted meat was eaten in winter, often in a stew.

Poor people ate a kind of **STEW** called pottage made from the peas, beans and onions that they grew. The only sweet foods the poor ate were the berries, nuts and honey that they collected from the woods. The rich ate fresh meat, such as

venison, chicken and goose. Inns served meals to travellers and large towns had takeaway food where you could buy 'hot thrush' or a 'hot sheep's foot'!

Many recipes from medieval times survive. Here is a medieval recipe for 'Puddyng of Purpaysse' (Stuffed Porpoise Stomach):

'Take the Blood of him, & the grease of him self, & Oatmeal, & Salt, & Pepper, & Ginger, & mix these together well, & then put this in the Gut of the porpoise, & then let it boil easily, & not hard, a good while; & then take him up, & broil him a little, & then serve forth.'

Servants prepared suckling pigs for the lord's table at a manor house.

Source – Recipe for Puddyng of Purpaysse (Harleian MS 279), England, c. 1430

Words to use in your project

banquet *(feast)*	**scullion** *(person who washed dishes and helped the cook)*	**spits** *(metal stick turned over fire to cook food)*
excavated *(dug up)*		
pitcher *(big cooking pot)*	**skillet** *(frying pan)*	**venison** *(deer meat)*

THE GREAT HALL

Rich people dined in the great hall – a large, high-ceilinged room. The lord and older relatives sat at the 'high table' where they were waited on by servants. Young children and others of a lower rank sat on benches at trestle **TABLES**. At each place, a servant would lay spoons, knives, cups and bread rolls – no forks. They ate from pewter or silver **PLATES** and goblets and most eating was done with the fingers, so pages carried around jugs of water and napkins. We know about the layout of later medieval halls from surviving buildings,

This 14th century great hall at Penshurst Palace, Kent is 62 feet long and 60 feet high.

such as the medieval Guildhall in London with its grand entrance hall built in 1411 and below-ground undercrofts.

CASE STUDY

Feasting was enjoyed by everyone on holy days.

Feasts

The Church set aside certain 'holy days' for feasts or festivals. On these days everyone had the day off work and took part in the celebrations. **FEASTS** were held outside or in the great houses and were prepared by many servants. Meals could have ten or more courses – and some had up to 100! People drank **BEER**, cider and wine. Feasts took a lot of planning and expense, as is clear in the following:

'And first: one hundred well-fattened cattle, one hundred and thirty sheep, also well fattened, one hundred and twenty pigs; and for each day during the feast, one hundred little piglets, both for roasting and for other needs, and sixty salted large well fattened pigs for larding and making soups.'

Eating and Drinking Glossary

archaeological	The study of history by digging up things from the past	**pewter**	Silver-grey metal made of tin and lead
goblets	Drinking vessels on stems	**porpoise**	Small-toothed whale
guildhall	Town hall	**pottage**	Stew made from peas, beans and onions
larding	Preparing animal fat	**undercroft**	The lowest floor of a medieval stone building, used for storage
pages	Medieval waiters		

See also: Town Life 8–9; Country Life 10–11; Health and Medicine 16–17; Trade and Craft 28–29

Source – Terence Scully, Du Fait de Cuisine par Maistre Chiquart, France, 1420

Health and Medicine

Men and women living in medieval times faced far more PAIN and SUFFERING than most people do today. The Church taught that by repenting to God, any illness would be cured. Other medical ideas were based on astrology. Doctors, apothecaries, nuns and midwives did their best to treat patients with herbs, simple operations and nursing care.

MEDICINE

Medieval **DOCTORS** used many different treatments. Some tried spells and charms or ointments made from dung, blood and animal fat.

Doctors believed that some **DISEASES** were caused because the patient had too much blood. So they made cuts in the patient's veins to let the 'extra' **BLOOD** drain away, or they put leeches on the body to suck out the blood. To cure headaches, **SURGEONS** sometimes cut a hole in the skull – a process called 'trephination'. A medical text had this advice on public health:

'Drinke not much wine, sup light, and soone arise, From care his head to keepe, from wrath his heart.'

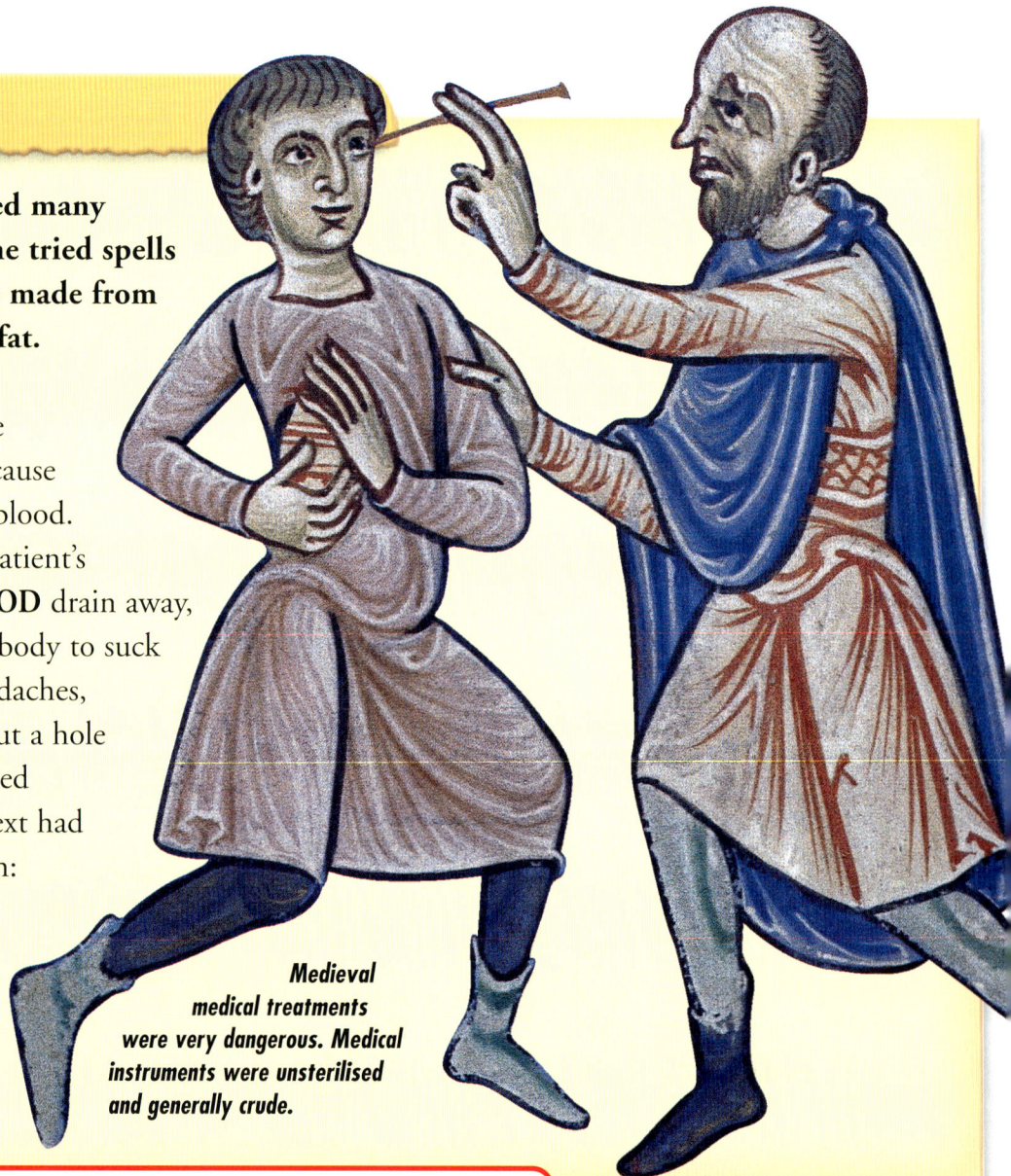

Medieval medical treatments were very dangerous. Medical instruments were unsterilised and generally crude.

Source – Salerno Book of Health, Italy, c. 11th century

Words to use in your project

ailments *(minor illnesses)*	**infection** *(virus, illness)*	**science** *(knowledge through study and experiments)*
astrology *(study of planets)*	**poison** *(deathly substance)*	
individual *(one)*	**remedy** *(cure)*	**symptoms** *(signs of illness)*

ALCHEMY

Alchemy was the first kind of **CHEMISTRY**. Alchemists believed that if certain substances were mixed together at certain temperatures, they could cure people. A lot of alchemists also believed that **MAGIC** played a part in healing the sick. Cures could be bought from alchemists, who would make up a cure after asking questions about the symptoms. The following describes the process of preparing the 'philosopher's stone' which was believed to cure anyone who was sick:

This illustration from a 14th century manuscript shows an alchemist teaching the secrets of alchemy to a pupil.

'Our dissolving water therefore carries with it a great tincture, and a great melting or dissolving; because that when it feels the vulgar fire, if there be in it the pure and fine bodies of sol or luna, it immediately melts them, and converts them into its white substance such as itself is, and gives to the body color, weight, and tincture.'

Source – Secret Book of Artephius, France, 12th century

Health and Medicine Glossary

alchemy	*Medieval chemistry – the preparing of chemicals to produce medicines*	**astrolabe**	*Medieval device for checking the positions of the stars and planets*
apothecary	*Person who prepares and sells medicines*	**melancholy**	*Sadness or depression*
		surgeon	*Doctor who treats patients by operating on them*
ascendent	*Rising – in astrology, the word is used to describe the movement of stars*	**tincture**	*Type of medicine*
		vulgar	*Lacking class or good taste*

See also: Religion 6–7; Death 12–13; Eating and Drinking 14–15; Men and Women 18–19

CASE STUDY

Astrology

People believed that the **STARS** and planets had a direct influence on their lives. Cures taken or formulas mixed up at particular times were believed to have better effect. For example, one medieval medical book records that:

'Saturn seems to have impressed the seal of melancholy on me from the beginning; set, as he is, almost in the midst of my ascendant Aquarius, he is influenced by Mars, also in Aquarius, and the Moon in Capricorn. He is in square aspect to the Sun and Mercury in Scorpio, which occupy the ninth house.'

Medieval astrologers used a device called an 'astrolabe' to find out things like when sunrise or sunset would fall and to work out the position of the Sun and stars in the sky.

Astrolabes such as this English one from 1326 were used for studying the stars and planets.

Source – Letter of Ficino to Giovanni Cavalacanti, quoted in Marsilio Ficino, Three Books on Life, Italy, 1489

Men and Women

Few people in medieval Europe could READ and WRITE and, because most of them were men, most information comes from men's viewpoints. When women married they usually spent most of their lives having and looking after children. Marriages usually lasted for life but that did not mean what it does for us today. Childbirth hazards and disease meant a marriage of 10–15 years was a long one since life expectancy was much shorter.

MARRIAGE AND CHILDREN

Among wealthy people, MARRIAGES were like business deals as wealth, position and political power mattered most.

Most wealthy people had their marriages arranged by their parents.

There were strict social codes that people were expected to follow. For example, it was outlined in the *Magna Carta* that:

'Heirs may be given in marriage, but not to someone of lower social standing. Before a marriage takes place, it shall be made known to the heir's next-of-kin.'

Young people usually married when they were between 12 and 15 years old. It also became fashionable for knights to choose a married woman and to love her from a distance. The knight would fight for her in battles and tournaments. This became known as 'courtly **LOVE**'. Having children was considered important in family life. Children in peasant families were more likely to help their parents at home than go to school. Most schools had no books and sometimes classes had as many as 100 students and the school day could be up to 13 hours long.

Source – Magna Carta, England, 1215

Words to use in your project

burnt at the stake *(tied to a pole over a bonfire, which was set alight)*   **captive** *(prisoner)*   **continents** *(main areas of land)*   **education** *(learning)*   **founded** *(set up)*   **matrimony** *(marriage)*   **university** *(college)*

FAMOUS PEOPLE

The tale of **ROBIN HOOD** is said to have been based on real characters. The earliest written version dates back to 1420. Here is an extract in the original Middle English language:

'But Robyn toke out a too-hond sworde, That hangit down be his kne; Ther as the schereff and his men stode thyckust, Thedurwarde wolde he.'

Christopher Columbus and Marco Polo were **EXPLORERS** who discovered other continents, including parts of Asia and America. Famous **WRITERS** include Christine de Pisan, who wrote many books of history and poetry. Geoffrey Chaucer was the most famous writer from the Middle Ages. He wrote his best-known book *The Canterbury Tales* in about 1386, which was one of the first books to be printed in England (over 100 years later).

The first written account of Robin Hood can be dated back to 1420.

Source – Robin Hood and the Monk, England, c. 1450. Translated into modern English, this passage would go something like this: 'Robin took out his two-handed sword, That hung down to his knees; And as the sherrif and his men stood strong, Robin rushed forward.'

Men and Women Glossary

Burgundians	Natives of Burgandy, France	**next-of-kin**	Closest living relative
executioner	Person who kills criminals who have been sentenced to death	**saints**	People regarded by the Church as holy after their death
faggots	Bundles of sticks	**tournaments**	Fights between knights on horseback in front of large crowds of people
heir	Person entitled to property of another after their death		

CASE STUDY

Joan of Arc was burnt at the stake for her beliefs. This image comes from a French book illumination from about 1420.

Joan of Arc

JOAN OF ARC was a French peasant girl who heard the voices of Christian saints. She ended up leading France to victory against England. But soon after, the Burgundians captured and sold her to the English. She was put on trial as a **WITCH** and was burnt at the stake. Joan is recognised today by the Catholic Church as a saint. Most of what we know about Joan of Arc comes from the official records of her trial in 1431. Troughout her trial, she insisted that she heard the voices of saints:

'... if I saw the fire lighted, the faggots prepared, and the executioner ready to kindle the fire, and if I myself were in the fire, I would not say otherwise, and would maintain to the death all I have said.'

Source – Transcripts of Joan of Arc's Trial, England, 1431

See also: Religion 6–7; Health and Medicine 16–17; Crime and Punishment 20–21 Penance and Pilgrimages 30–31

Crime and Punishment

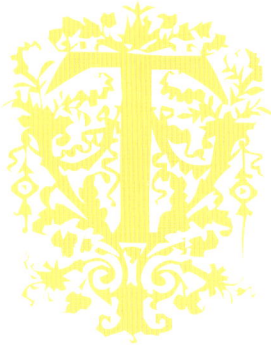

There was a court system in the Middle Ages, through which most convicted criminals would be punished by fines. However, punishments could also be violent and cruel. There were very few prisons and a serious crime would often result in the death penalty. When the COURTS could not decide if someone was guilty or not, it was left for God to decide in the form of a judicial ordeal.

COURTS AND TRIALS

A peasant who had been hanged might be left hanging on a gibbet as a warning to others. This illustration comes from a German manuscript of 1480.

If poor people were caught BEGGING, they would be put in the stocks. Thieves had their hands cut off and violent crimes were punished by BEHEADING or hanging.

Most towns had a gibbet outside where people who had been hanged were left to rot. We know where gallows were located from placenames that still exist today, such as: 'Dead Man's Oak' or 'Gallows Hill'. 'Judicial ordeal' involved the person on trial being made to suffer a punishment that normally involved fire or boiling water. The judicial ordeal was banned by the church in 1215. In 1232, the Inquisition was set up to hunt out those who disagreed with the teachings of the Catholic Church. Anyone found guilty by the Inquisition might be TORTURED:

'... the inquisitor ordered that, dressed in a short tunic, the prisoner be put first in a bath of hot water, then of cold. Then, with a stone tied to his feet, he was raised up again, kept there for a while, and dropped again, and his shins were poked with reeds as sharp as swords.'

Source – Angelo Clareno, An Inquisitional Torture Session, Italy, 1304

THE PEASANTS' REVOLT

In the summer of 1381, revolts broke out in some parts of England after the introduction of poll **TAX**. The rebels went to London where they killed church ministers. Then the Mayor of London killed the peasant leader, Wat Tyler. An account from the time described the event like this:

'*And the Mayor went thither and found him, and had him carried out to the middle of Smithfield, in presence of his fellows, and there beheaded. And thus ended his wretched life. But the Mayor had his head set on a pole and borne before him to the King ...*'.

Hundreds of **PEASANTS** died, but later governments remembered the revolt and gave peasants a fairer deal.

This illustration shows the execution of Archbishop Simon of Sudbury and Sir Robert Hales at Tower Hill in 1381.

Source – Anonimalle Chronicle, English Peasants' Revolt, England, 1381

Crime and Punishment Glossary

ballad	*Song that tells a story*	poll tax	*A tax on the people*
beheading	*Death by having head cut off*	revolts	*Trying to overthrow the king or people in power*
Inquisition	*Church hunt for heretics*	stocks	*Wooden clamp for arms, neck and sometimes feet, positioned in the centre of a town or village*
judicial ordeal	*Church-led group that tried people accused of crimes against God*		
manorial court	*The court of the manor*		

CASE STUDY

The Battle of Bosworth Field was recorded by many medieval writers and artists.

Killing of a King

In August 1485, two English armies confronted each other at Bosworth Field in England. One was led by Richard III, the other by Henry Tudor, Earl of Richmond. Two hours later the king's army was defeated, Richard was dead and his **CROWN** lay in a thorn bush. Lord Stanley picked it up and placed it on Henry Tudor's head. A ballad by an eye-witness described the moment:

'*... the crowne of gold that was bright, to the Lord Stanley deliuered itt bee. Anon to King Henery deliuered it hee ... & said, "methinke ye are best worthye to weare the crowne and be our King".*'

He was now Henry VII, King of England.

Source – Anonymous, Ballad of Bosworth Field, England, late 16th century

See also: Power 4–5; Town Life 8–9; Death 12–13; Men and Women 18–19

21

The Crusades

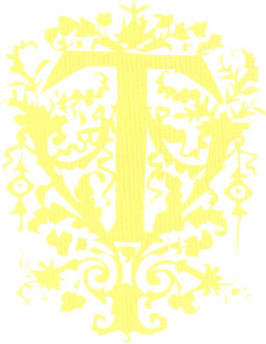

The Crusades were WARS where Christians tried to recover the city of Jerusalem and the holy land of Palestine, which had become part of the Muslim empire. Eight main Crusades took place from 1095, until the Muslims finally drove the Christians out in 1291. Overall, the Crusades were not a success for the Christians but contact with Arab civilisations taught the Europeans many new things about building and warfare. They also discovered carpet, sugar and learned about stars, mathematics and medicine.

CRUSADERS AND SARACENS

Crusaders came from all over Europe. Some joined bands of 'fighting monks', such as the KNIGHTS of St John or the Knights Templar.

Crusaders were Christian soldiers who fought to win the 'Holy Land' (Jerusalem and Palestine) from the Muslims.

The Muslim **SOLDIERS** of the holy land were called Saracens and included Arabs, Turks and Kurds. Their most famous leader was Saladin who earned the respect of many Crusaders. His capture of **JERUSALEM** in 1187 started the bloody Third Crusade, led by Richard I. A source from the period described the Third Crusade like this:

'Arrows fell like raindrops, so that one could not show a finger above the ramparts without being hit. There were so many wounded that all the hospitals and physicians in the city were hard put to it just to extract the missiles from their bodies.'

Finally, in 1229, the Emperor Frederick II of Germany recovered Jerusalem. Rather than fight the Saracens, he made peace with them and persuaded the Sultan to surrender the holy city. Jerusalem remained in European hands for 15 years but was lost completely in 1244. On the whole, the Crusades were a costly failure for the Europeans.

Source – Anonymous, *The Capture of Jerusalem by Saladin*, England, 1187

JEWS, CHRISTIANS AND MUSLIMS

Jews were persecuted for being anti-Christian throughout the Middle Ages.

Although most of Europe was **CHRISTIAN**, **MUSLIM** lands stretched from parts of Spain through North Africa to Central Asia. There were communities of **JEWS** in many parts of Europe too as the Romans had expelled their ancestors from Jerusalem in 70 AD. In most of Christendom, religious **HATRED** against Muslims and Jews was high. Jews had been treated terribly in England and in 1290 Edward I expelled them. A medieval writer named Albert of Aix wrote this about the Christian attacks on Jews:

'... *they rose in a spirit of cruelty against the Jewish people scattered throughout these cities and slaughtered them without mercy.*'

Source – Albert of Aix, Emico and the Slaughter of the Rhineland Jews, France, 1096

The Crusades Glossary

Arabs	Natives of Arabia
Christendom	Places where Christians lived
Crusades	A series of wars launched by Europeans against the Arabs to establish Christian rule in the Muslim-controlled territory of the Holy Land
Crusaders	Christian military men who fought to regain the Holy Land from the Muslims
depopulated	Not many people living there
Muslims	Followers of the Islamic religion
physicians	Doctors
sultan	Muslim ruler
truce	Agreement to stop fighting

See also: Power 4–5; Religion 6–7; Death 12–13; Buildings 26–27

Richard the Lionheart

In 1189, Richard I became King of England and the next year he joined the Third Crusade. During the war, Richard became very ill and decided to accept Saladin's peace terms. A source described the situation:

'*As his illness became very grave, the King ... chose, as the least inconvenient course, to seek to make a truce rather than to desert the depopulated land altogether and to leave the business unfinished as all the others had done who left the groups in the ships.*'

Even though the Crusade was unsuccessful, Richard was loved by his people. His heroic actions brought him the nickname 'Coeur de Lion' (Lionheart).

Richard I was considered a hero by his subjects.

Source – Anonymous, Richard the Lionheart Makes Peace with Saladin, England, 1192

23

Art

Medieval art is usually divided into two overlapping periods: Romanesque (1050–1180) and Gothic (1150–1550). These names describe the different creative STYLES and methods. Most medieval ARTISTS were either monks or craftspeople. They rarely signed their works because they made things to honour God or royalty. They believed that the person who made the works of art was not important.

ART FOR THE CHURCH

This painting is called the 'Wilton Diptych' and was painted in about 1395. It shows Richard II worshipping the Virgin Mary and infant Jesus.

Most art (particularly metalwork and sculpture) was created for the Church. Church leaders, kings and noblemen hired artists to produce pictures, statues and other works to teach people about Christianity.

Painters painted scenes from the Bible on the walls of churches, while sculptors carved scenes on columns, walls and doors or made statues of holy figures. Metalworkers made chalices, plates and crosses and glassworkers produced colourful STAINED-GLASS WINDOWS for the church. Frightening scenes in the artworks encouraged people to be good Christians (or they would go to Hell) while expensive materials made them realise the importance and power of God. Surviving records of the art owned by churches include the Chantry Certificates of 1547. The Chantry Certificates list all the objects belonging to private chapels.

Words to use in your project

adornment (decoration)
icons (pictures of the Holy Family or saints)
illuminations (colourful letters)
plaster (thick substance to make walls smooth)
sculptor (person who makes statues)
technique (methods)

MATERIALS AND METHODS

To make **PAINT**, artists had to grind pigments and then mix them with resin, water, egg yolk or oil. Many recipes for making paint survive, such as this one for making the colour red:

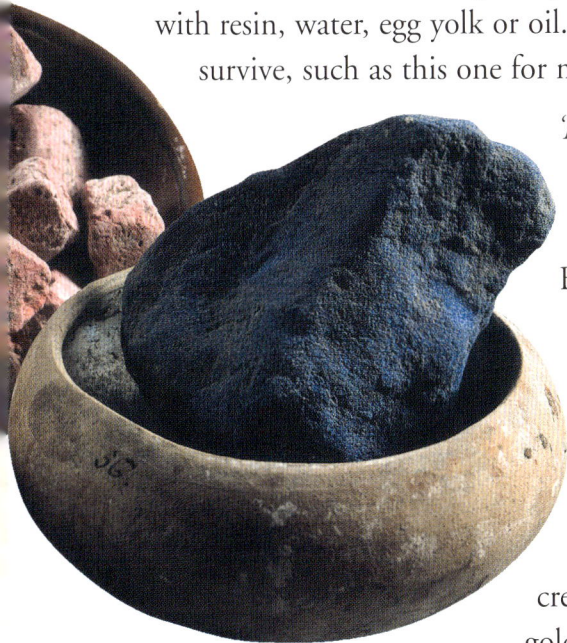

'Mingle salt and honny together in a bason, let it stand eight daies, then seeth it, and it will be a red colour.'

Brushes were made out of animal hair or fur that was tied to the quill of a feather or wooden stick. **SCULPTORS** and woodworkers used stone, wood or marble to make statues. Other craftspeople created with glass, ivory, enamel, gold, silver and bronze, or made tapestries, embroideries or stained-glass windows. Clay was used for making pottery or tiles.

Paint was made from grinding pigments like these during the Middle Ages.

Source – A Booke of Secrets, England, 1596 (translated from Dutch edition of 1531)

Art Glossary

chalice	A wine cup used in Mass		from animals, plants, earth or rocks and used to make paint or dye
embroideries	Art that involves stitching pictures into cloth		
enamel	Coloured liquid that becomes smooth, shiny and hard after heating	**quill**	Pen made from a feather
		resin	A liquid made from tree sap
frescoes	Pictures painted on wet or damp plaster	**seeth**	Boil gently
		tapestries	Thick fabrics, which are woven with threads (the Bayeux Tapestry is actually an embroidery!)
illuminations	Illustrations from medieval handwritten books		
pigments	Coloured materials taken		

See also: Religion 6–7; Buildings 26–27; Trade and Craft 28–29; Penance and Pilgrimages 30–31

CASE STUDY

This detail from the Baueux Tapestry shows William of Normandy's ships sailing towards Hastings.

Storytelling Art

Most people in medieval times could not read. Pictures were an important way of telling **STORIES**. Much of the art of the time told stories from the **BIBLE**. One kind of painting that was especially important was the illuminations that were created to illustrate books. Paintings on church walls, called 'frescoes' were also popular. The Bayeux Tapestry is one of the most famous pieces of medieval art because it told the story of William the Conqueror, Harold II and the Battle of Hastings of 1066. Today the Bayeux Tapestry is located in Normandy, France.

Source – You can see details from the Bayeux Tapestry on the Internet at: http://hastings1066.com/baythumb.shtml

Buildings

Some of the techniques used for building are still used by architects and builders today. Masons and architects designed fine buildings – including churches, castles, great houses and monasteries. The medieval ST PAUL'S CATHEDRAL, with its towering wooden steeple, was the main landmark of the city of London and the tallest building in Europe. Medieval towns needed strong walls and well-guarded gates to keep attackers out. Most houses didn't stay standing longer than 50 years.

HOUSES

Most HOUSES were made of wooden frames with walls made of wattle and daub. After about 1400, many rich people lived in large brick houses with wooden-panelled interior walls.

By the end of the medieval period, these houses had large chimneys and occasionally glass windows. Peasants lived in simple timber-framed houses with wattle and daub walls with only one or two rooms. **FLOORS** were of bare earth, windows had shutters but no glass, and there were no chimneys. **FIRES** were lit on stone or tile hearths in the centre with a hole above for smoke. Many town houses had upstairs rooms that overhung the streets. The floors of great buildings were tiled or strewn with rushes or straw, and rugs and carpets were designed as coverings for tables or chests. Masons, woodcarvers and stonecarvers decorated these buildings inside and out with carvings and statues on the walls and interior ceilings.

This 16th century manuscript illustration shows carpenters making a wooden frame for a house in about 1430.

Words to use in your project	adorned (decorated)	elaborate (detailed)	a castle, great house or town)
	bailey (outer wall of a castle)	keep (castle tower)	motte (mound)
	dwelling (house)	moat (deep ditch around	structure (building)

CASTLES

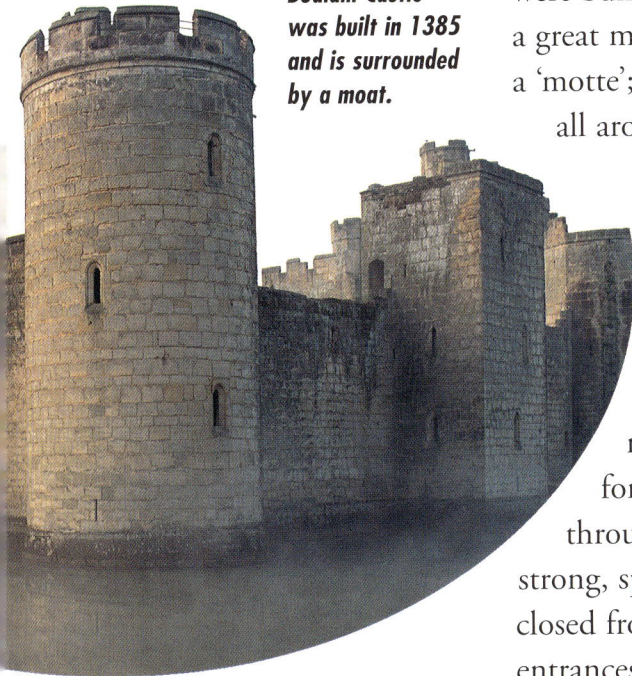

Bodiam Castle was built in 1385 and is surrounded by a moat.

When William I first took control of Britain, his Norman barons built strong **CASTLES** as fortresses. The earliest castles were built of wood, often on a great mound of earth called a 'motte'; with a deep ditch all around. By the 12th century, many castles had massive stone **TOWERS** (keeps) surrounded by high walls up to 10 metres thick. Windows were narrow slits, too small for attackers to squeeze through and 'portcullises' - strong, spiked drop-gates that closed from above, protected entrances. The outsides of castles were probably whitewashed and often brightly painted, with coloured roof tiles, so they weren't just stone-coloured as we see them today.

Buildings Glossary

arches	Curved structures that serve as openings or supports to the building	interior	Inside
		masons	People who cut, shape and build in stone and brick
architects	People who design buildings	monasteries	Place where monks live
buttresses	Thick stone or brick piers built against the outside of a wall to strengthen it	rushes	Straw scattered on the floors. Sometimes herbs and sweet-smelling flowers were added
fortresses	Buildings that have been strengthened against attack	strewn	Scattered untidily
hearth	Area surrounding a fireplace		

CASE STUDY

Churches

Many churches and **CATHEDRALS** built in Europe during the medieval period were built in the Romanesque style (1050–1180). These had rounded **ARCHES** above windows and doors. Romanesque churches were built in the shape of a cross. Gothic-style churches were built from about 1180 until the 16th century. Buttresses replaced the heavy pillars of Romanesque churches, with pointed arches rather than round ones. The interior walls of churches were painted in rich colours, such as blues and reds, and patterned with things like stars or swirls. All this, as well as huge stained-glass windows made these churches seem filled with light and air. Statues and paintings also decorated the interior.

This stained-glass window from Chartres Cathedral in France was made in the 13th century.

See also: Power 4–5; Religion 6–7; Town Life 8–9; Country Life 10–11

Trade and Craft

We know a lot about the trades and crafts of the early medieval period because in 1086, William I sent officials all around England to find out what jobs people did. All the INFORMATION was written down in a great book, called the *Domesday Book*. Trading with foreign countries was very important, but TRAVEL was difficult and dangerous. Merchants travelled across the sea, where they had to be careful of pirates. Even the ships themselves which weren't safe in rough seas.

TRADES AND CRAFTS

The people who practised a craft usually sold their goods also. But many people made a living simply through trading alone.

Spinning and weaving were crafts that were generally done by women.

These tradesmen and merchants, like craftspeople, lived and worked near markets. Most trades across Europe were controlled by powerful groups of merchants, called 'guilds'. The largest of these, the 'Hanseatic League', was formed in the 12th century mainly by German merchants. Henry III gave them permission to set up a base in London. Their ships brought salted fish, timber, dyes and iron goods. In return, they bought English **GOODS** and sold them abroad. Most crafts- and tradespeople belonged to guilds. Guilds would fine anyone making or selling shoddy goods, or anyone whose **PRICES** were too high. Here is an example of a rule from the Weavers' guild:

'But if any one be caught with false cloth, his cloth will be burned publicly, and verily, the author of the crime will amend according to justice.'

Source – *The Regulations of the Weavers' Gild of Stendal, Germany, 1233*

Words to use in your project

cogs (merchants' sailing ships)
export (take to sell in another country)
import (bring in to a country)

guildhalls (places where the guilds met)

information (knowledge)
survey (find out about people in society)

SHIPS AND SAILING

Many medieval towns built waterfronts where ships could dock to unload cargo.

Sailing **SHIPS** carried goods to and from other countries. Many towns built big timber waterfronts out into rivers so that **CARGO** ships could dock there. Travel improved relationships between countries and people soon became familiar with foreign produce that they had never seen before. We know from written accounts that it was much cheaper for people to transport goods by water than overland in the Middle Ages. The rights of merchants were protected by many rules like this one:

'*Also we decree that if a laden ship should come up the Rhone and should wish to moor at any wharf on the river bank of Arles, then the men of that ship may remove on their own authority, and moor elsewhere, without contradiction, any empty ship which may be without a cargo...*'.

Source – Port of Arles: The Navigation Code, France, 1150

Trade and Craft Glossary

authority	Power or right to give orders and control others		people of England in 1086
cargo	Goods carried on a ship	**guilds**	Group that made sure the standard of crafts and trades was good
contradiction	Statement or opinion that disagrees with another	**manuscripts**	Books written by hand
decree	Official order or law	**movable**	
Domesday Book	A record of the lands and	**type**	Individual letters that can be moved about

The first printing press in England was set up by William Caxton in 1476.

Books

In medieval times, **BOOKS** (or manuscripts) were written out by hand, usually by monks – a slow and expensive process. Then, in 1450, a German named Johannes Gutenberg produced the first printed Bible. The craft of paper-making had come to Europe from the East and this, along with **PRINTING**, made books much cheaper to produce. In 1471 an Englishman, William Caxton, learned about the new 'movable type' printing, which had been invented in Korea. He set up his own printing press in Westminster in 1476 and printed copies of nearly 100 different books.

You can see an original Gutenburg Bible on the British Library's website at: http://prodigi.bl.uk/gutenbg/default.asp

See also: Town Life 8–9; Country Life 10–11; Eating and Drinking 14–15; Art 24–25

Penance and Pilgrimages

The medieval church taught that people should confess their SINS to a priest. If they were truly sorry, then God would FORGIVE them. The priest might then give them a penance – which could be anything from saying a prayer, to helping others, to going on a pilgrimage. A pilgrimage is a journey to a HOLY place. People also went on pilgrimages to ask for special favours or simply to give thanks to God. Flagellants were a group of people who punished themselves so that God would forgive their sins.

PILGRIMS

PILGRIMS followed special trails across Europe and the Middle East to visit places where important religious events had taken place.

Sometimes pilgrims paid money to see SHRINES. Shrines were believed to have special POWERS, especially the power of healing. They often contained the bodies of saints or bits of their bone, hair or clothing. One of the most famous accounts of a medieval pilgrimage was Geoffrey Chaucer's *The Canterbury Tales*. Here is an extract:

'It happened that, in that season, on a day; In Southwark, at the Tabard, as I lay; Ready to go on pilgrimage and start; To Canterbury, full devout at heart; There came at nightfall to that hostelry; Some nine and twenty in a company; Of sundry persons who had chanced to fall; In fellowship, and pilgrims were they all!; That toward Canterbury town would ride.'

Pilgrims were people who went on a special trail to a holy place to seek God's forgiveness for their sins.

Source – Geoffrey Chaucer, The Canterbury Tales, England, Late-14th century

FLAGELLANTS

This detail from a 15th century Italian painting shows flagellants kneeling in prayer.

Some people punished themselves as a way of being closer to God. They walked about in groups, singing psalms and lashing themselves with **WHIPS**. They said that this was punishment not just for their own sins, but for the sins of the world. These people became known as flagellants. A source from the period described flagellants in this way:

'They formed circles and beat upon their backs with weighted scourges, rejoicing as they did so in loud voices and singing hymns suitable to their rite and newly composed for it ... They flogged their shoulders and arms, scourged with iron points so zealously as to draw blood.'

Source – Jean de Venette, France, 1349

CASE STUDY

The Canterbury Tales

In his poem, *The Canterbury Tales*, Chaucer wrote about a group of pilgrims travelling to **CANTERBURY**. It is a very long poem and draws attention to the foolishness of human nature. Characters in the group included a merchant, a knight, a nun and a ploughman. One of the pilgrims, the Wife of Bath, had been on many pilgrimages, as described in this extract:

'Three times she'd journeyed to Jerusalem; And many a foreign stream she'd had to stem; At Rome she'd been, and she'd been in Boulogne, In Spain at Santiago, and at Cologne.'

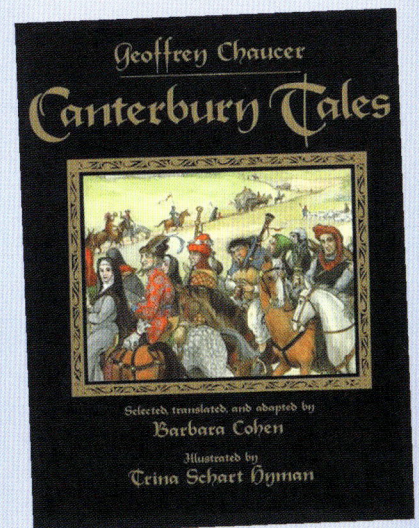

Chaucer's famous book, The Canterbury Tales.

Source – Geoffrey Chaucer, The Canterbury Tales, England, Late-14th century

Penance and Pilgrimages Glossary

devout	Deeply religious	psalms	Religious songs
flagellants	People who beat themselves for religious reasons	rite	Religious act or ceremony
		scourges	Whips used for punishment
penance	Religious punishment for sins	shrines	Holy places, usually devoted to a saint
pilgrims	People who travel to holy places	zealously	Very enthusiastically or obsessively

See also: Religion 6–7; Men and Women 18–19; Art 24–25; Trade and Craft 28–29

Index

MEDIEVAL TIMELINE

1066
William of Normandy invades and conquers England. King Harold is killed at the Battle of Hastings and William is crowned king.

1086
The Domesday Book is completed. It contains statistics about the people of England – their jobs and land.

1096
First Crusade begins. The Crusaders were Christian armies from all over Europe who fought to regain lands (Palestine and Jerusalem) captured by the Muslims.

1141
Period of Anarchy when Matilda and her cousin Stephen fight over the crown. Stephen eventually wins.

1147
Second Crusade begins. This Crusade is a failure for the Christians.

1154
Henry II is king – the first of a long line of Anglo-French kings.

1162
Thomas Becket is made Archbishop of Canterbury and is killed for his belief that the Church should rule over the King.

1189
Richard the Lionheart becomes King of England. Third Crusade begins. King Richard makes a deal with Saladin and certain privileges are granted to Christians.

1202
Fourth Crusade begins. The Crusaders never reach the holy land. Instead, Europeans begin trading their goods with exotic goods from Arab countries.

1215
King John of England is forced to add his seal to the 'Magna Carta' or Great Charter – a set of rules to ensure the king ruled his people in a just way.

1291
The end of the Crusades.

1348
The black plague sweeps Europe killing one out of every three people.

1381
The Peasants' Revolt occurs in England.

1387
Geoffrey Chaucer begins writing The Canterbury Tales.

1429
Joan of Arc leads France to defeat England. She is burned at the stake in 1431.

1485
Henry Tudor defeats and kills Richard III and becomes King of England.